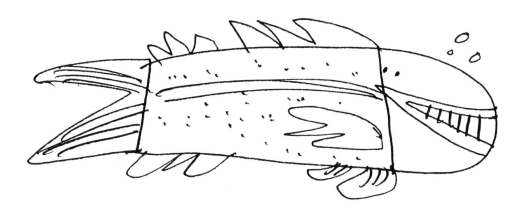

Get Ready for
THE CODE

A PRIMER FOR THE **Explode The Code** SERIES/BOOK A

Nancy Hall

Educators Publishing Service, Inc.
Cambridge and Toronto

Cover Design by Hugh Price

Educators Publishing Service, Inc.

31 Smith Place, Cambridge, Massachusetts 02138

Printed in U.S.A.   ISBN 0-8388-1780-7   May 2002 Printing

Color the one that is different.

Trace the letter **f** with your finger. This letter has the sound you hear at the beginning of 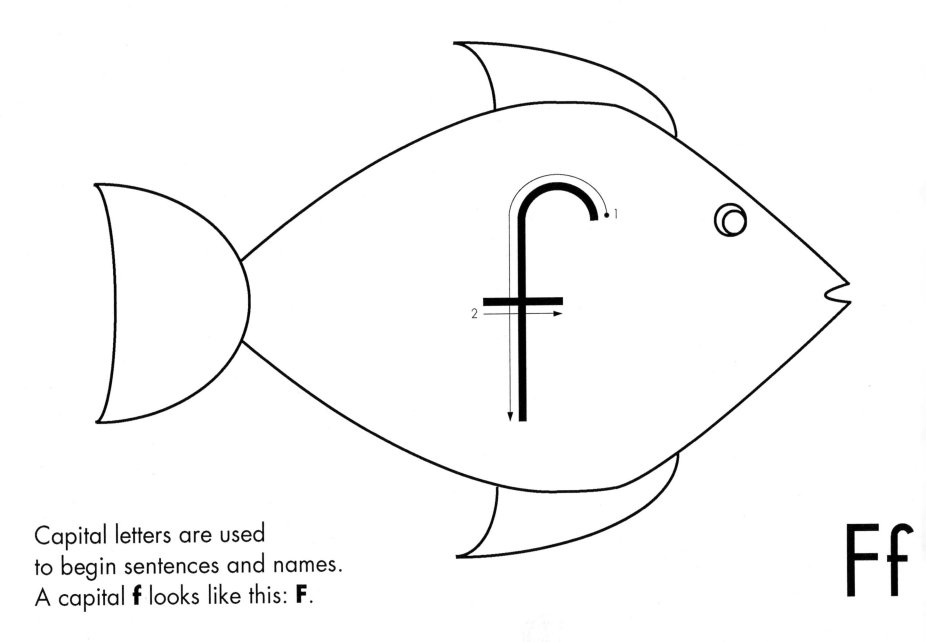. Say the sound.

Capital letters are used
to begin sentences and names.
A capital **f** looks like this: **F**.

Ff

Follow the path from the **f** to the picture whose name begins with /**f**/. Say the sound. Try not to cross any lines.

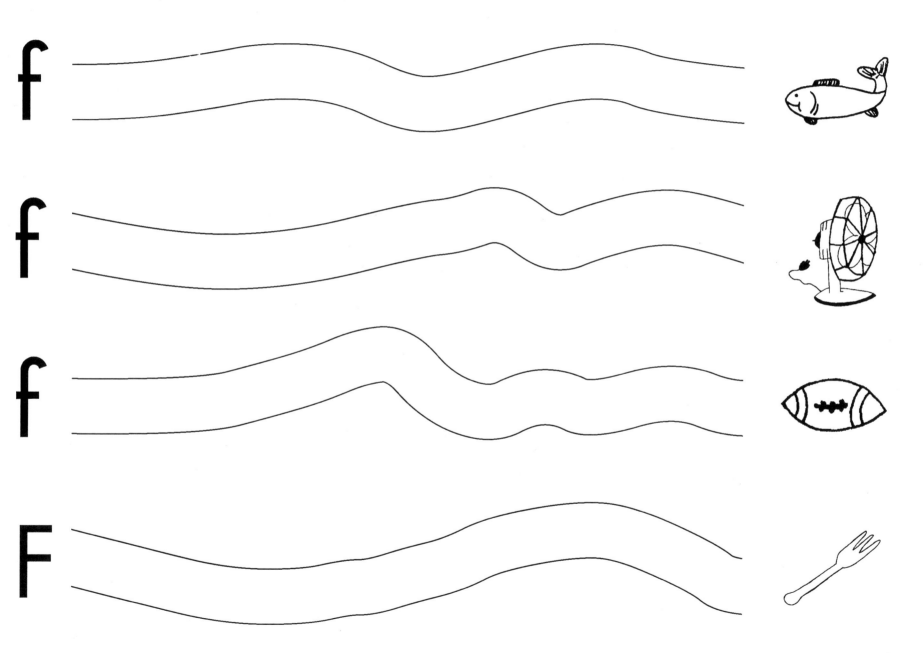

Look carefully at the letter in the box. Circle the letters that match it.

f	s f b f f

f	b h f t f

f	i f l f h

f	f k t l f

F	L F K F H

Say the name of the picture. Now say the sound that comes at the beginning of 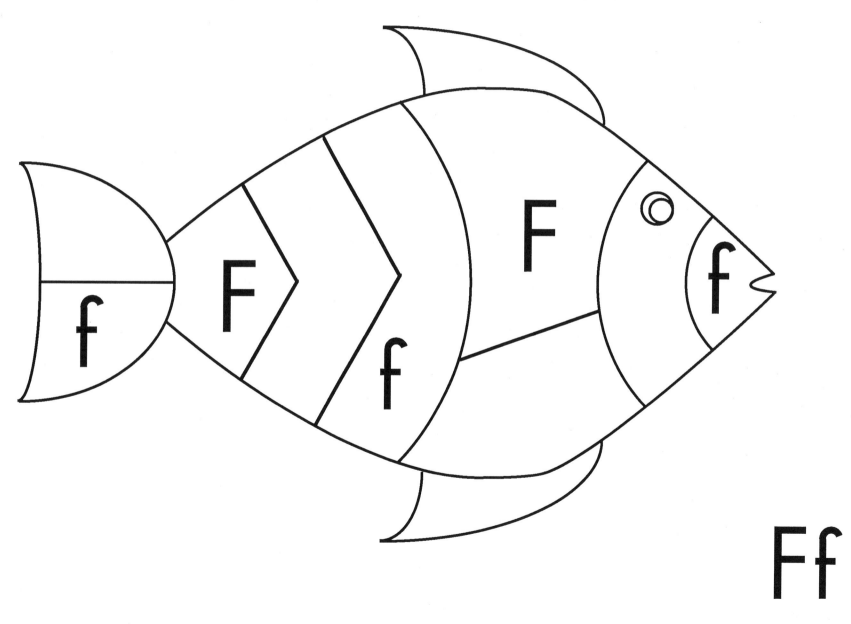 . Color only the sections with the letter **f** or **F** in them.

Ff

Teacher: Read the directions aloud while the students listen and work on page 7.

1. I am thinking of something that is often made of wood. It keeps animals in a yard or field. What is it? What sound does **fence** begin with? Color the **fence**.

2. I am thinking of something that you plug in. It moves the hot air and makes you feel cooler. What is it? What sound does **fan** begin with? Draw a circle around the **fan**.

3. Now find a picture of something that we use when we eat. What is it? What sound do you hear at the beginning of **fork**? Draw an X on the **fork.**

4. I am thinking of something that lives in water and swims with its fins. What is it? Say the sound at the beginning of **fish**. Color the **fish** many colors.

5. I am thinking of a part of the body that is attached to your leg. You each have a left one and a right one. What body part is it? What sound does **foot** begin with? Draw a shoe on the **foot**.

6. Now I am thinking of something I like to do. To do it, I need a rod, a hook, and some bait. It is fun to go _____. Have you ever gone **fishing**? What sound do you hear at the beginning of **fishing**? Draw a fish on the girl's line.

7. I am thinking of something you kick with your foot. You can run with it and score a touchdown. What is it? What sound does **football** begin with? Color the stripes on the **football**.

8. The last picture shows a part of the hand. You can wiggle it. What is it called? What sound does **finger** begin with? Draw a box around the **finger**.

Listen; then follow the directions.

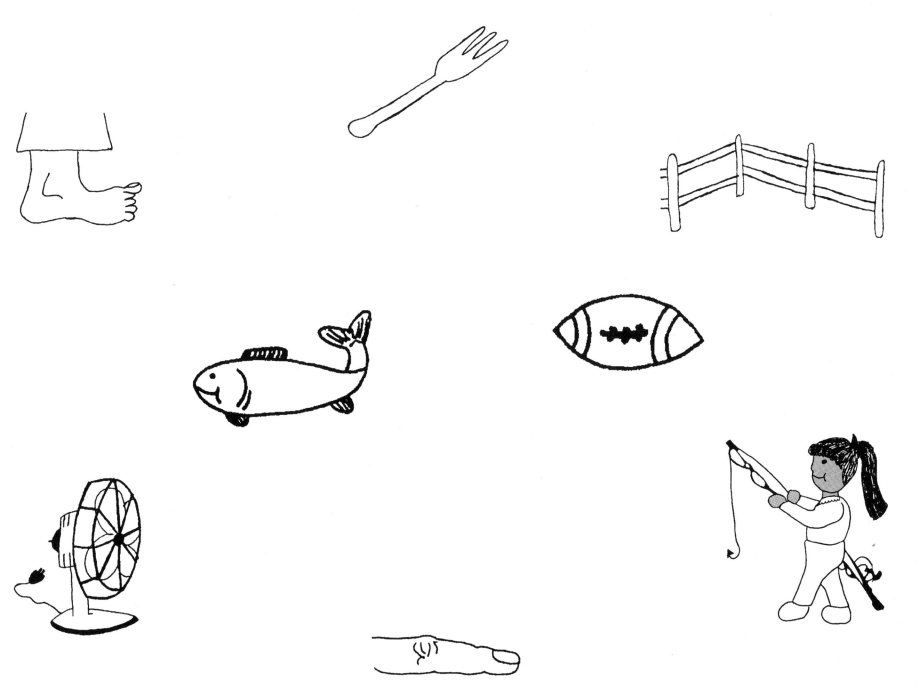

f says /f/ as in 🐟. On each line color the picture whose name begins with **f**.

f		
f		
f		
f		
f		

Follow the arrows to write the letter **f**, which says /**f**/ as in . Say the sound aloud.

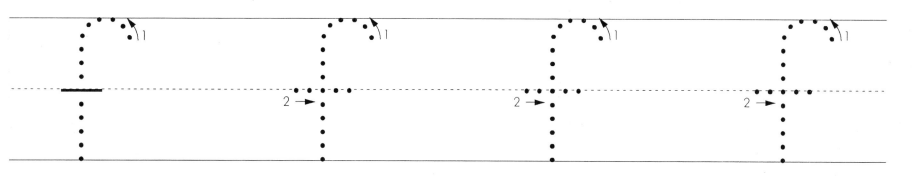

Notice that **f** is two spaces tall. Trace the letters.

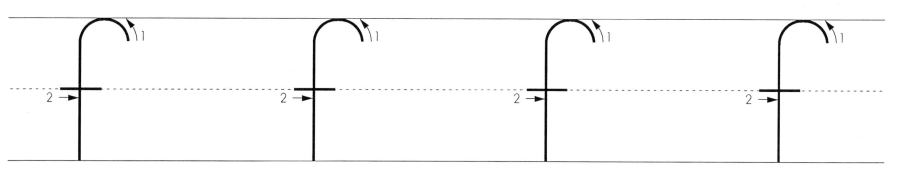

9

begins with /**f**/. "X" each picture whose name begins with /**f**/.

f	(fork)	(dog)	(box)
f	(car)	(pig)	(finger)
f	(fence)	(house)	(television)
f	(fishing)	(bed)	(hat)
f	(ball)	(bus)	(foot)

Trace the letters.

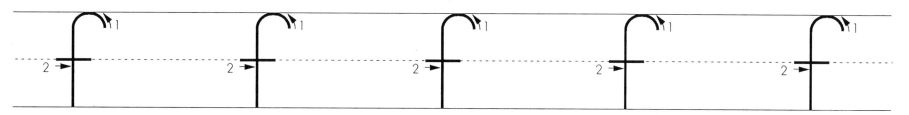

Copy the letter.

"X" each picture whose name begins with **f**. Write **f** below those pictures.

  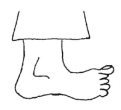  

11

Say the name of the picture and the sound of its first letter.	Find the letter. Circle it.	Write the letter.
	l f t	
	o i f	
	f m t	
	k f l	
	r l f	

Color the one that is different.

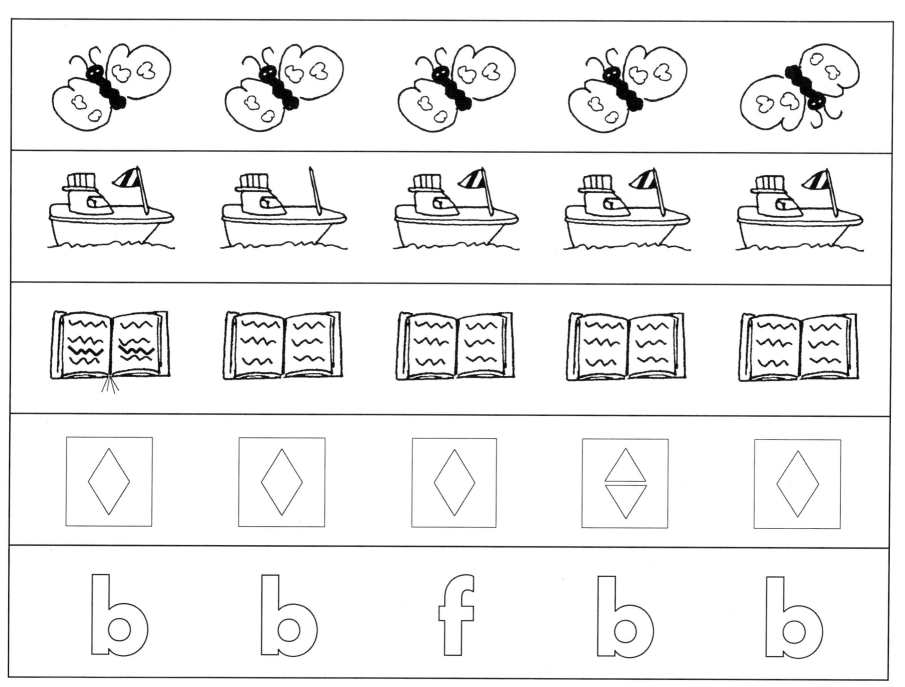

Trace the letter **b** with your finger. This letter has the sound you hear at the beginning of . Say the sound.

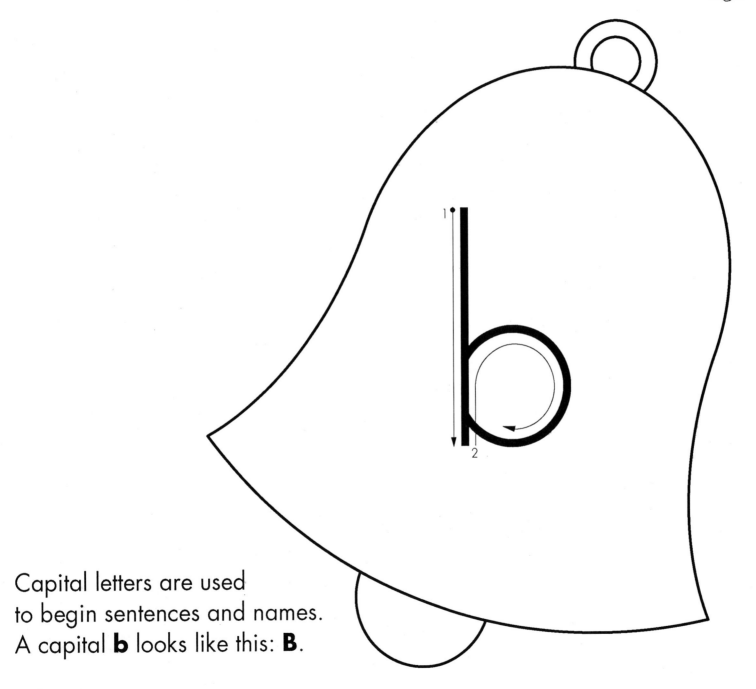

Capital letters are used
to begin sentences and names.
A capital **b** looks like this: **B**.

Bb

Follow the path from the **b** to the picture whose name begins with /**b**/. Say the sound. Try not to cross any lines.

Look carefully at the letter in the box. Circle the letters that match it.

b	f	b	t	l	b

b	b	l	f	b	t

b	k	t	b	b	f

b	f	b	b	k	b

B	P	B	C	B	F

Say the name of the picture. Now say the sound that comes at the beginning of . Color only the sections with the letter **b** or **B** in them.

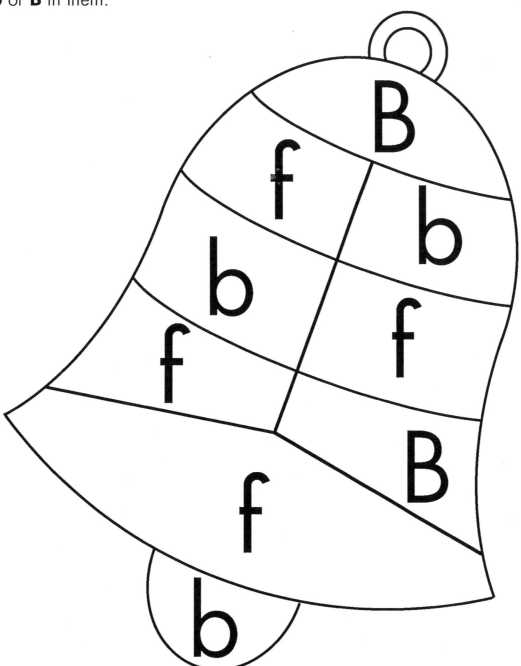

Bb

Teacher: Read the directions aloud while the students listen and work on page 19.

1. I am thinking of something you wear on your feet to keep them dry. What are they called? What sound do you hear at the beginning of **boots**? Color the **boots**.

2. I am thinking of something you buckle around your waist to hold your pants up. What is it? What sound do you hear at the beginning of **belt**? Draw an X on the **belt**.

3. I am thinking of something that is filled with air. It will burst if you prick it. What is it? What sound does **balloon** begin with? Color the **balloon** your favorite color.

4. I am thinking of something that has a handle, which makes it easy to carry many things. (But please do not try to carry water in it.) What is it called? What sound do you hear? Draw a circle around the **basket**.

5. I am thinking of something you can ride, but you must push the pedals to make it go. What is it? What sound do you hear at the beginning? Draw a box around the **bicycle**.

6. Now I am thinking of something big you can sit inside to ride someplace. It is big. Lots of children go to school on a school _____. Say the word again. What sound does **bus** begin with? Color the **bus** its usual color.

7. I am thinking of something that you can put things in. It has a lid so the things won't fall out. It is made of cardboard. What is it called? What sound do you hear at the beginning of **box**? Color the lid of the **box**.

8. The last picture is of something with wings. It builds a nest to lay its eggs in. What is it? You may color this **bird** any color you like, but do it carefully.

Listen; then follow the directions.

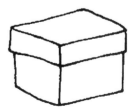

Draw a line from the box to each picture whose name begins with /**b**/ as in .

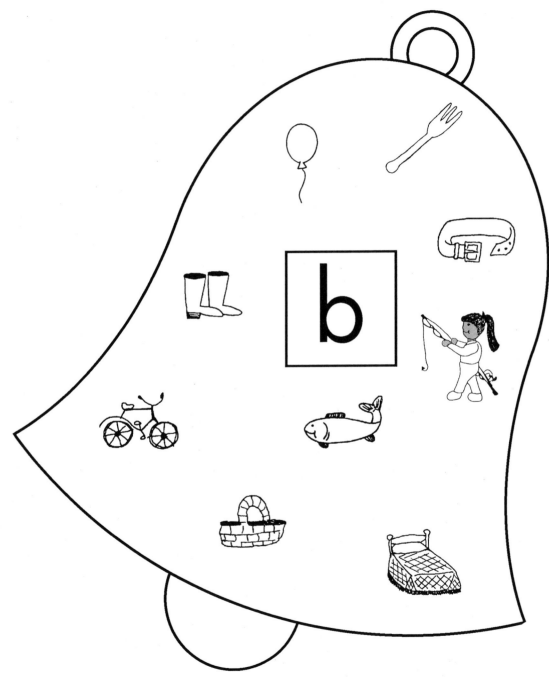

Follow the arrows to write the letter **b**, which says /**b**/ as in . Say the sound aloud.

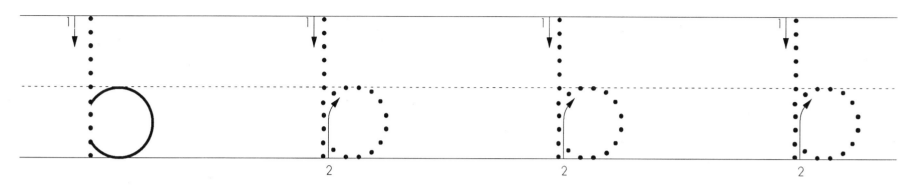

Notice that **b** is two spaces tall. Trace the letters.

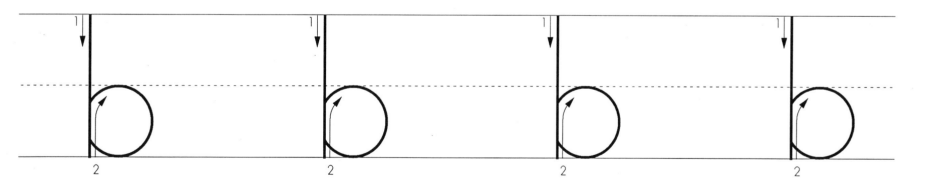

21

Which letter does the picture's name begin with? Circle it.

Trace the letters.

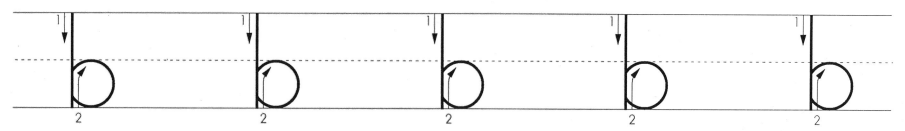

Copy the letter.

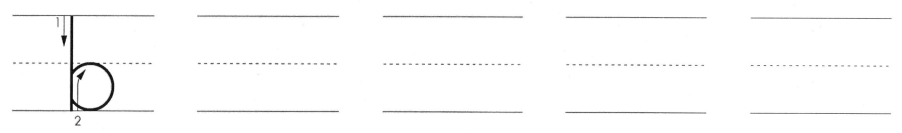

"X" each picture whose name begins with **b**. Write **b** below those pictures.

 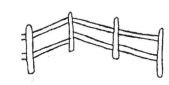   

23

Which sound does the word begin with? Write the letter that stands for the sound.

Color the one that is different.

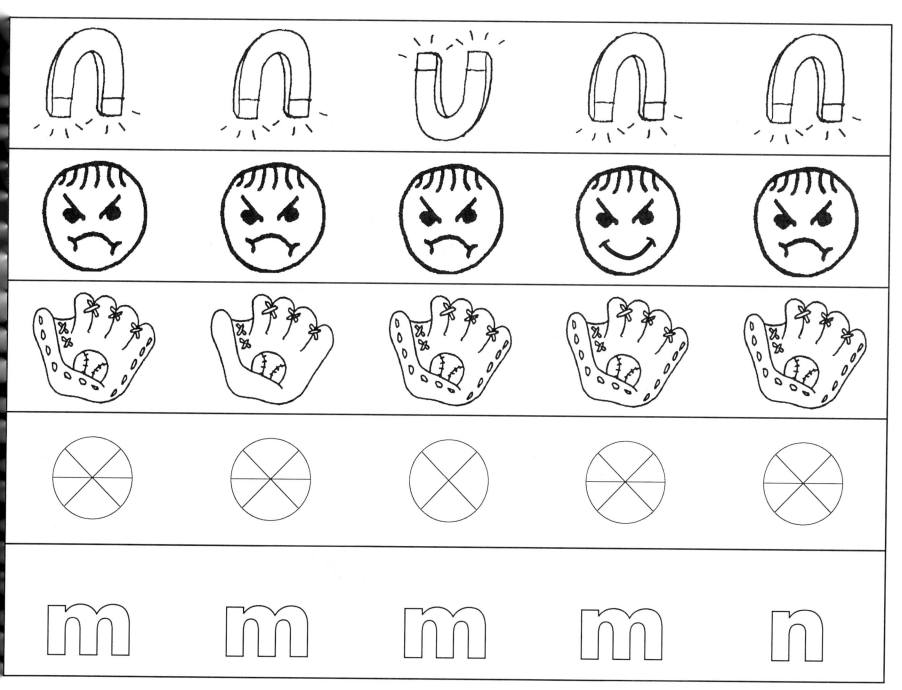

25

Trace the letter **m** with your finger. This letter has the sound you hear at the beginning of . Say the sound.

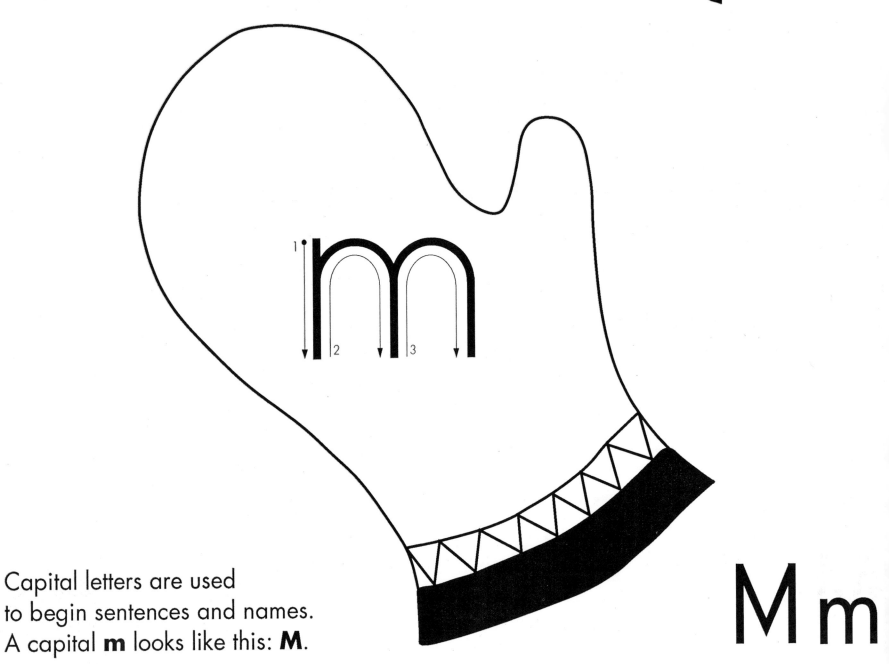

Capital letters are used
to begin sentences and names.
A capital **m** looks like this: **M**.

M m

Follow the path from the **m** to the picture whose name begins with /**m**/. Say the sound. Try not to cross any lines.

27

Look carefully at the letter in the box. Circle the letters that match it.

| m | b | m | h | m | n |

| f | f | b | l | f | t |

| m | m | h | m | b | m |

| b | b | l | b | h | o |

| M | N | K | M | N | M |

Say the name of the picture. Now say the sound that comes at the beginning of . Color only the sections with the letter **m** or **M** in them.

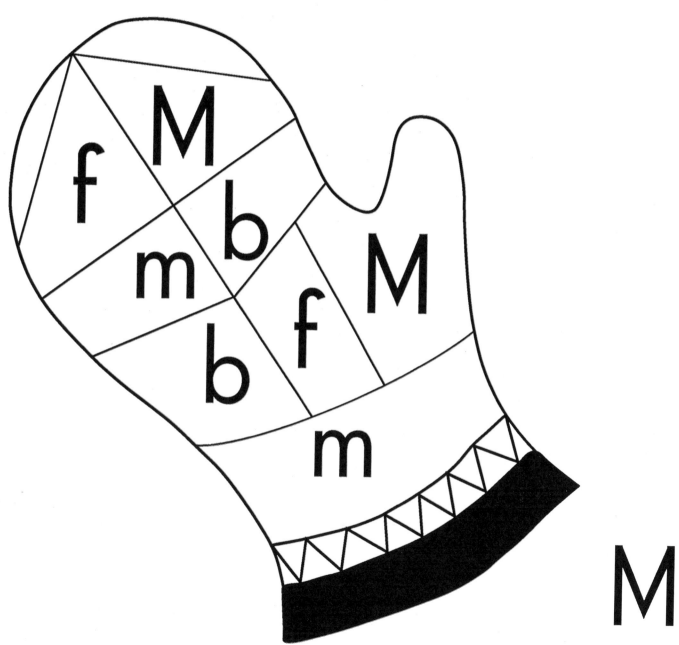

Mm

Teacher: Read the directions aloud while the students listen and work on page 31.

1. I am thinking of something you can use to buy things. You keep it in your purse or wallet or sometimes in a bank. What is it? What sound do you hear at the beginning of **money**? Draw a square around the **money**.

2. I am thinking of a clever animal that uses its fingers and toes to swing in trees. It also likes to eat bananas. What animal am I thinking of? What sound do you hear at the beginning of **monkey**? Color the **monkey**.

3. I am thinking of something that glows brightly in the sky at night. Astronauts walked on it. What is it? What sound do you hear at the beginning of **moon**? Color the **moon** yellow.

4. Find the picture that shows something you put on your hands to keep them warm in winter. You should wear these when you make snowballs. What are they called? Say the sound you hear at the beginning of **mittens**. Draw a circle around one **mitten**.

5. Now I am thinking of something adults use to light a fire or a candle. What is it called? What sound does **match** begin with? Draw an X on the **match**.

6. The creature in this picture looks terrible and makes you feel afraid. We call this a /m/_____. What sound do you hear at the beginning of **monster**? Draw a box around the **monster**.

7. This picture shows something very, very high. When we climb to the top of one of these, we can see a long way. What do we call this tall thing? What does **mountain** begin with? Color the **mountain** green.

8. Find the picture we have not talked about. This is a picture of a small animal that sometimes gets into cupboards and chews holes in boxes of food. It also likes to eat cheese. It squeaks and runs fast when it sees you. Its name begins with the /m/ sound. What is its name? Color the **mouse** any way you like.

Listen; then follow the directions.

Draw a line from the tag to each picture whose name begins with /**m**/ as in .

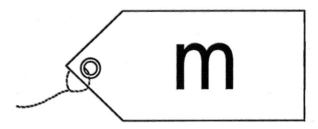

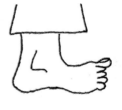

Follow the arrows to write the letter **m**, which says /**m**/ as in . Say the sound aloud.

Trace the letters.

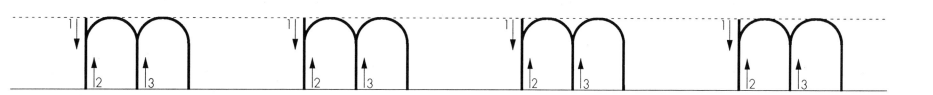

Color each picture whose name begins with **m** as in

m		
m		
m		

Trace the letters.

m m m m m

Copy the letter.

m

"X" each picture whose name begins with **m**. Write **m** below those pictures.

Which letter does the picture's name begin with? Circle it.

Say the name of the picture and the sound of its first letter.	Find the letter. Circle it.	Write the letter.
	f m b	
	b f m	
	m b f	
	b f m	
	m f b	

37

Which sound does the word begin with? Write the letter that stands for the sound.

Color the one that is different.

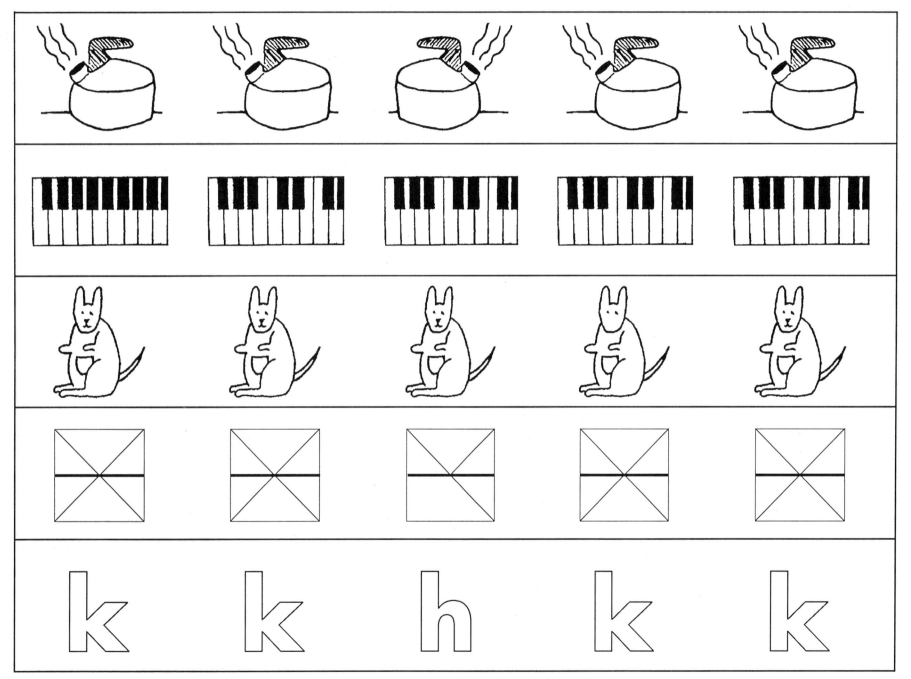

Trace the letter **k** with your finger. This letter has the sound you hear at the beginning of 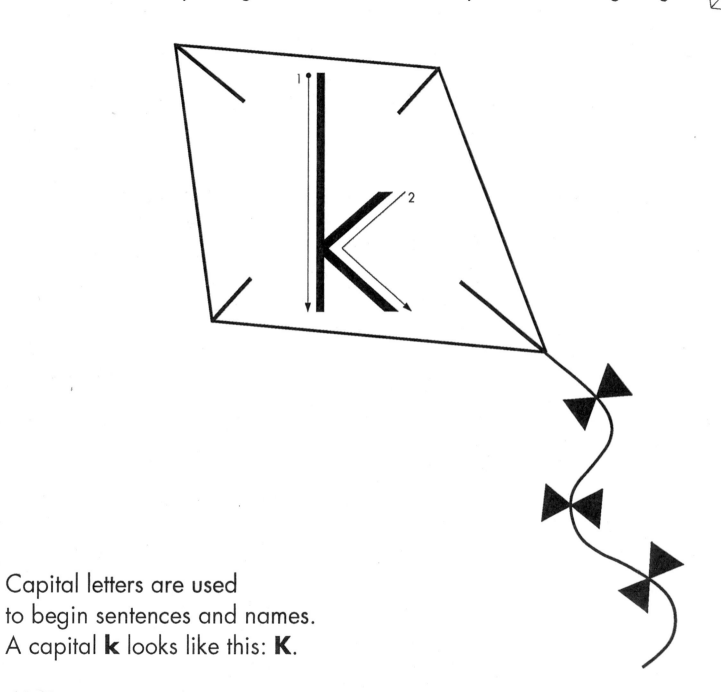 . Say the sound.

Capital letters are used
to begin sentences and names.
A capital **k** looks like this: **K**.

Kk

Follow the path from the **k** to the picture whose name begins with /**k**/. Say the sound. Try not to cross any lines.

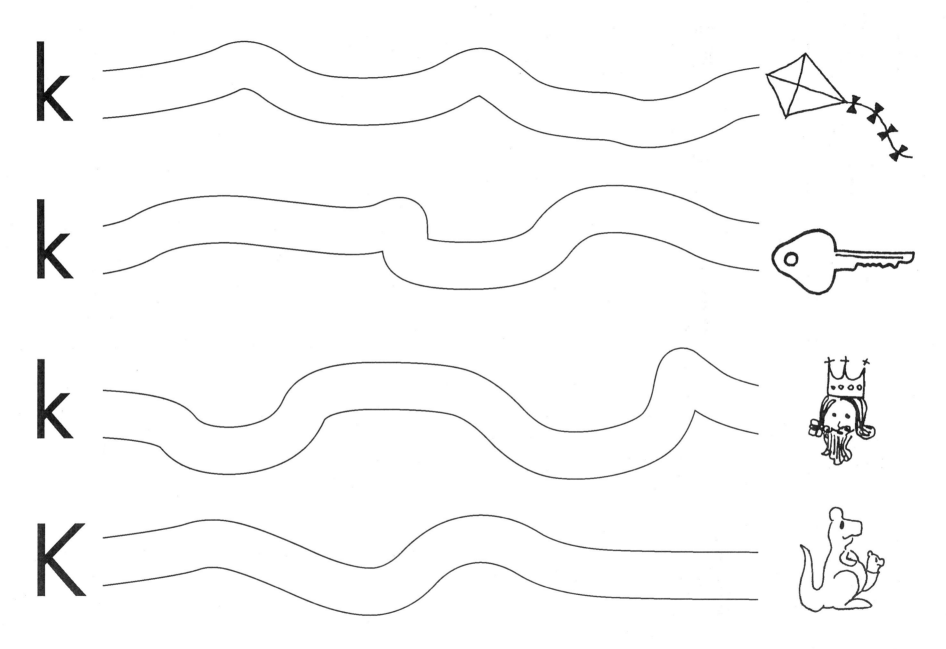

Look carefully at the letter in the box. Circle the letters that match it.

| k | b | k | f | k | k |

| f | f | t | k | f | l |

| k | k | f | x | f | k |

| m | n | b | m | w | m |

| K | M | K | V | K | K |

42

Draw a line from each 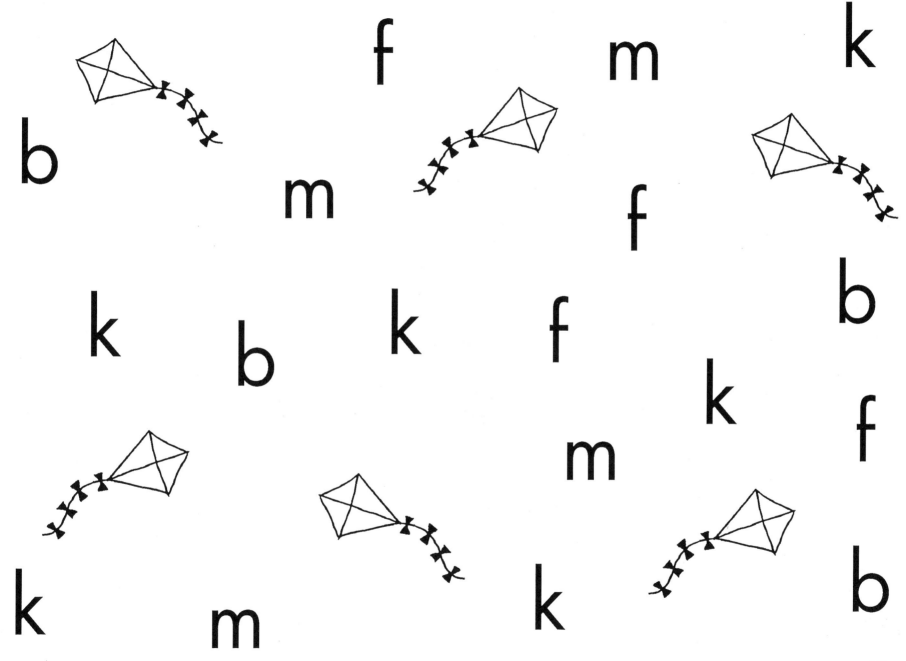 to the letter **kite** begins with.

f

m

k

b

m

f

b

k

k

b

f

k

m

f

m

k

b

43

Teacher: Read the directions aloud while the students listen and work on page 45.

1. I am thinking of something you use to unlock a door. It is made of metal and fits in a small hole. What is it? What sound do you hear at the beginning of **key**? Color the **key**.

2. I am thinking of something that is fun to do with a ball. You use your foot to do this. What is it called? What sound do you hear at the beginning of **kick**? Draw a circle around the ball.

3. I am thinking of something that can go up high in the sky if there is a lot of wind. But be sure you hold on to the string! What is it? Draw a longer tail on the **kite**.

4. I am thinking of an animal that lives in Australia. The mother carries her baby in her pouch. When she takes big hops, the baby stays safe inside the pouch. What animal am I thinking of? What sound does **kangaroo** begin with? Color just the tail of the **kangaroo**.

5. I am thinking of something small and soft and fluffy. It makes a tiny mewing noise when it is hungry. What is the name for a baby cat? What sound does **kitten** begin with? Draw a collar on the **kitten**.

6. I am thinking of a person who wears a crown and sits on a throne. This man is a _____. What sound does **king** begin with? Draw a circle around the **king**.

7. The picture we have not talked about yet shows two people who like each other. They are puckering up their lips to give each other a big _____. What sound does **kiss** begin with? Color this picture any way you wish.

Listen; then follow the directions.

45

Draw a line from the box to each picture whose name begins with /**k**/ as in :

k

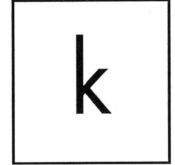

Follow the arrows to write the letter **k**, which says /**k**/ as in . Say the sound aloud.

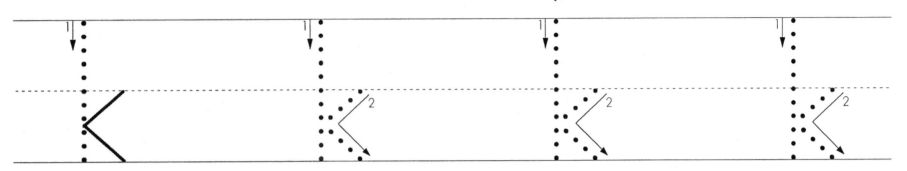

Notice that **k** is two spaces tall. Trace the letters.

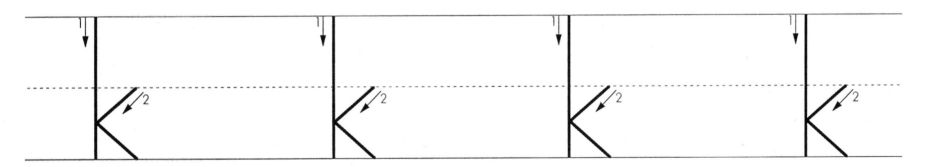

Color each picture whose name begins with **k** as in .

k		
k		
k		

Trace the letters.

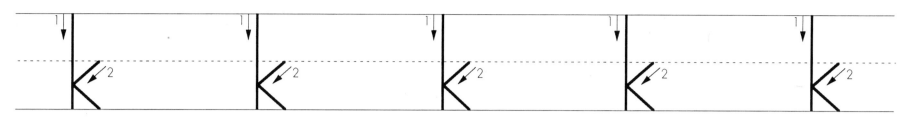

Copy the letter.

"X" each picture whose name begins with **k**. Write **k** below those pictures.

Draw a line from each picture to the letter that begins its name.

f

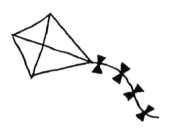

k

b

m

k

b

Say the name of the picture and the sound of its first letter.	Find the letter. Circle it.	Write the letter.
	b f k	
	m f k	
	k b m	
	b m k	
	f b k	

Which sound does the word begin with? Write the letter that stands for the sound.

Color the one that is different.

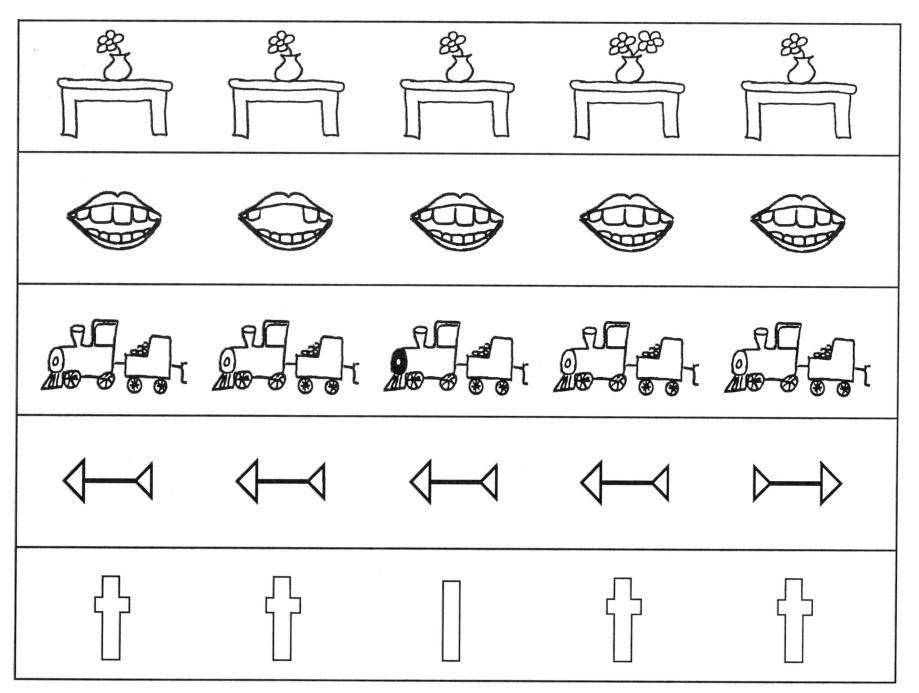

Trace the letter **t** with your finger. This letter has the sound you hear at the beginning of . Say the sound.

Capital letters are used
to begin sentences and names.
A capital **t** looks like this: **T**.

T t

Follow the path from the **t** to the picture whose name begins with /t/. Say the sound. Try not to cross any lines.

Look carefully at the letter in the box. Circle the letters that match it.

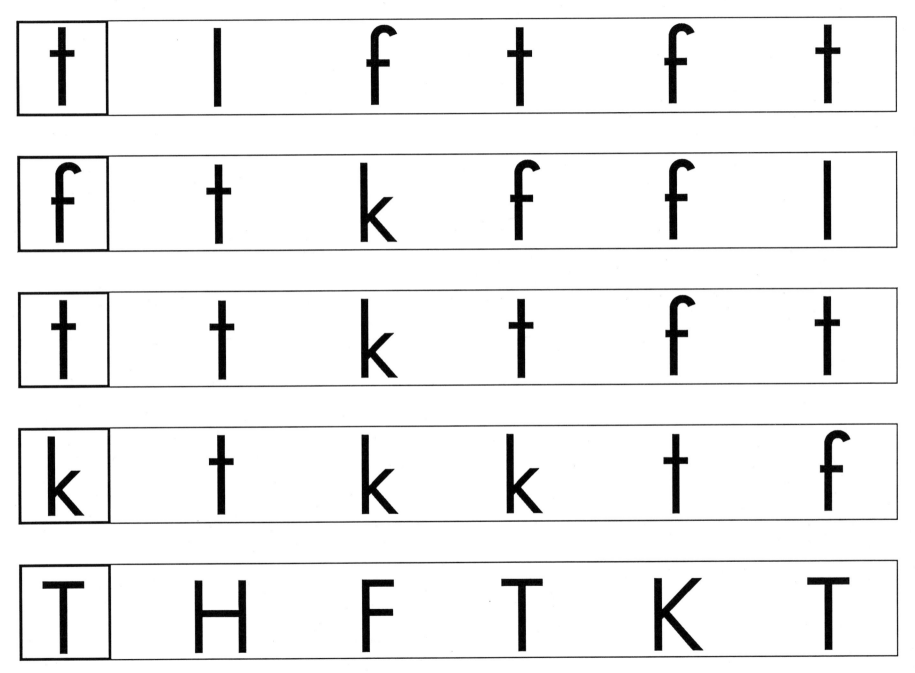

Draw a line from each 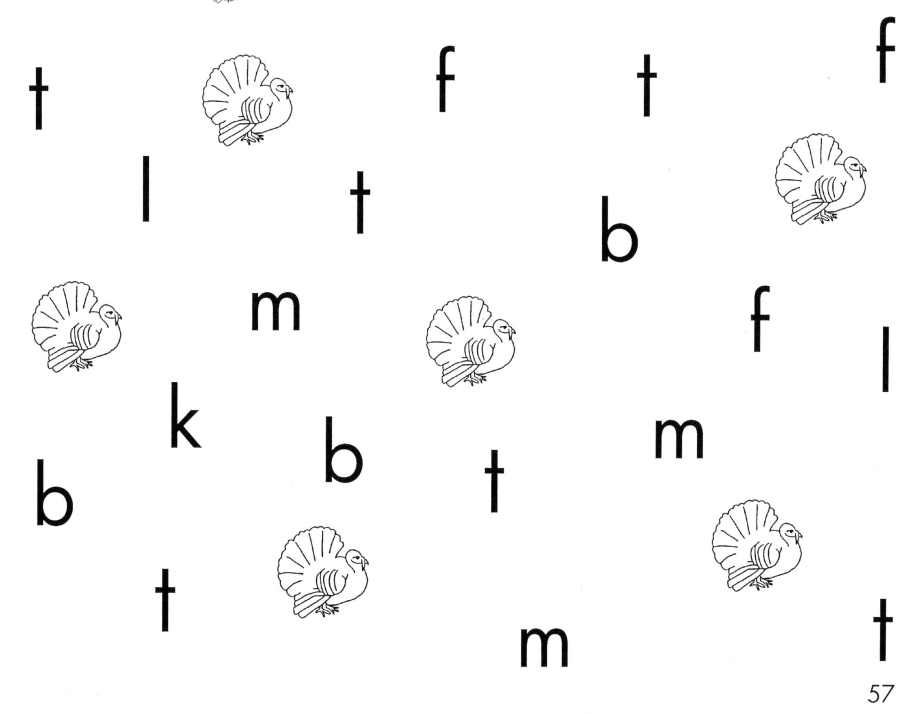 to the letter **turkey** begins with.

t

f

t

f

l

t

b

m

f

l

k

b

m

b

t

t

m

57

Teacher: Read the directions aloud while the students listen and work on page 59.

1. I am thinking of something that you use to clean your teeth. It has a handle with a brush at the end. What is it? What sound do you hear at the beginning of **toothbrush**? Draw toothpaste on the **toothbrush**.

2. I am thinking of a part of the body. A person's foot has five of these. Say the word. What sound do you hear at the beginning of **toe**? Color the toenail only.

3. I am thinking of something that you use to talk with someone far away. You hold the receiver next to your ear to listen. What is it? Say the sound you hear at the beginning of **telephone**. Draw a circle around the **telephone**.

4. Many animals have these. Horses and cows swish theirs to keep the bugs and flies away. Dogs wag theirs when they're happy to see you. What am I thinking of? What sound do you hear at the beginning of **tail**? Draw an X on the **tail**.

5. I am thinking of an animal that moves very slowly. It is protected by a hard shell. What animal am I thinking of? What sound does **turtle** begin with? Color the **turtle**.

6. I am thinking of something you sleep in when you go camping. It has two flaps for doors and is often held up by poles and rope. What is this thing called? What sound do you hear at the beginning of **tent**? Draw another rope to make the **tent** stronger.

7. I am thinking of something that you use in the kitchen. It makes toast by heating bread until it's crisp. What is it called? Draw a piece of toast coming out of the **toaster**.

8. The last picture is of something that you can turn on and off. You can watch your favorite programs on it. What is its name? What sound does **television** begin with? Draw something on the **television** screen.

Listen; then follow the directions.

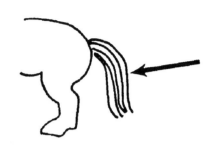

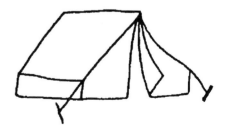

Draw a line from the tag to each picture whose name begins with /t/ as in .

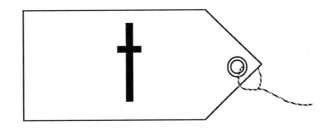

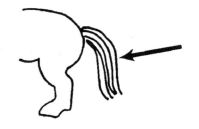

60

Follow the arrows to write the letter **t**, which says /**t**/ as in . Say the sound aloud.

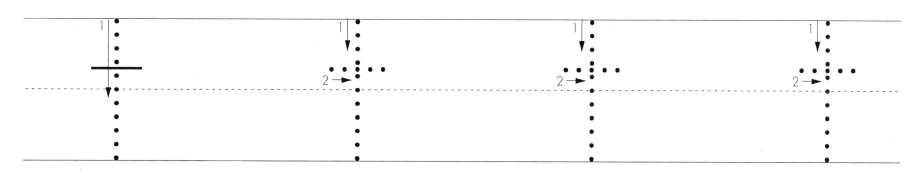

Notice that **t** is two spaces tall. Trace the letters.

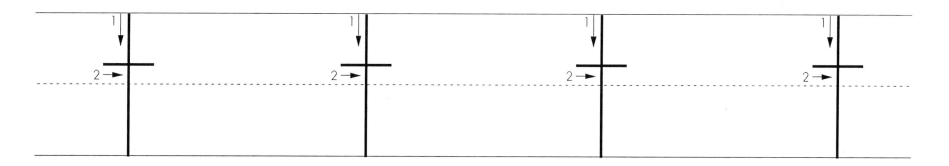

Draw a line from the picture to the letter that begins its name.

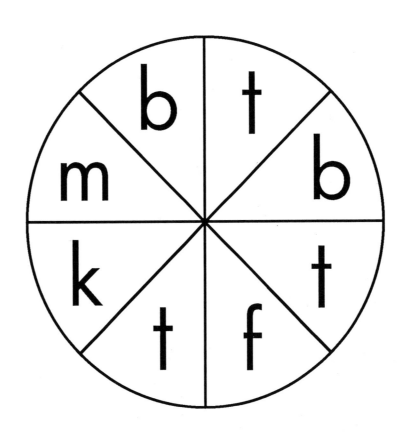

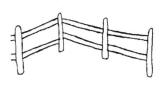

62

Trace the letters.

Copy the letter.

"X" each picture whose name begins with **t**. Write **t** below those pictures.

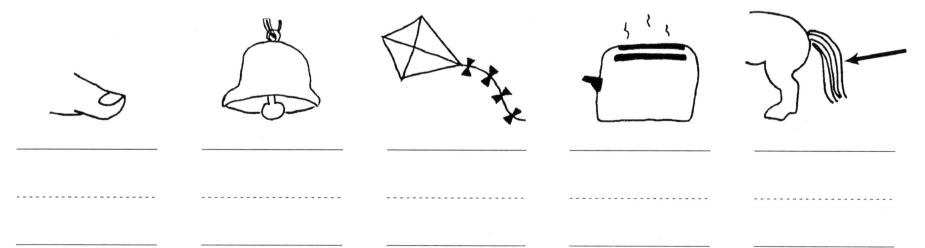

63

Which sound does the word begin with? Write the letter that stands for the sound.

Color the one that is different.

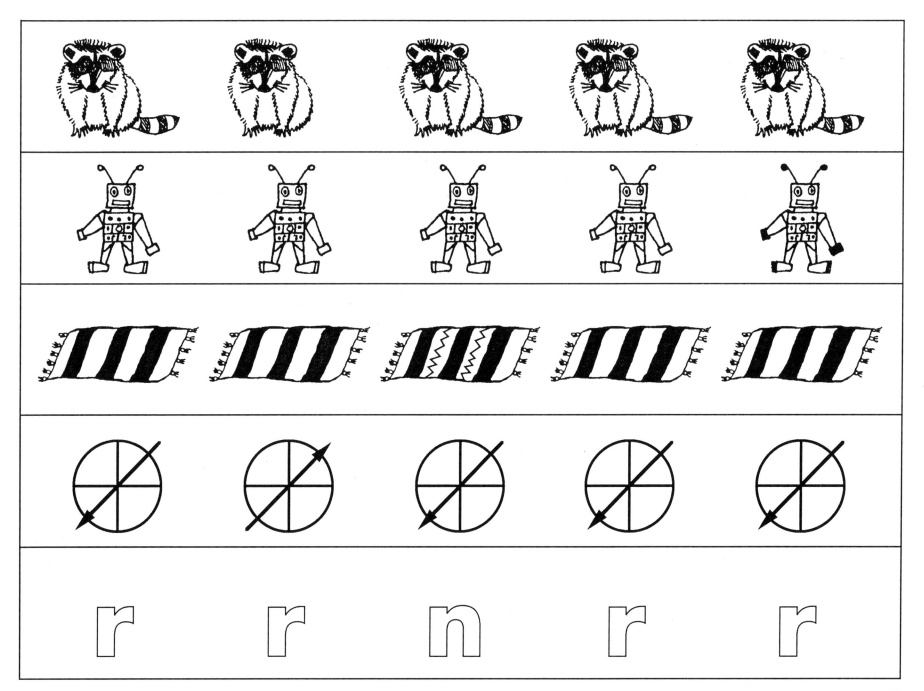

Trace the letter **r** with your finger. This letter has the sound you hear at the beginning of . Say the sound.

Capital letters are used
to begin sentences and names.
A capital **r** looks like this: **R**.

R r

Follow the path from the **r** to the picture whose name begins with **/r/**. Say the sound. Try not to cross any lines.

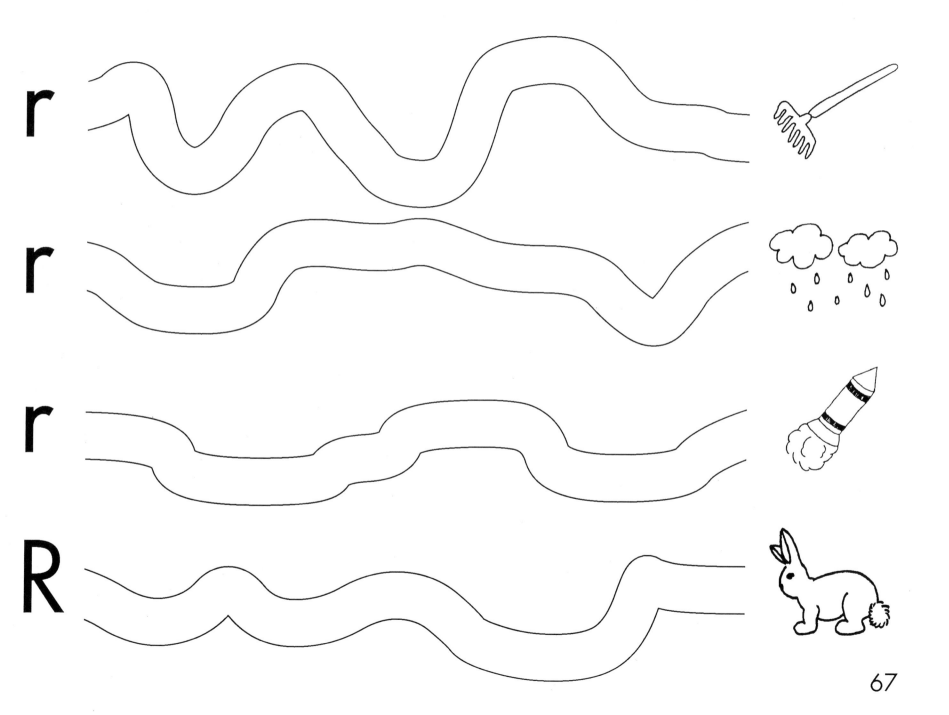

Look carefully at the letter in the box. Circle the letters that match it.

| r | n | r | c | r | m |

| k | x | k | f | t | k |

| r | r | m | r | n | r |

| t | k | t | f | l | t |

| R | P | R | F | R | B |

Say the name of the picture. Now say the sound that comes at the beginning of . Color only the sections with the letter **r** or **R** in them.

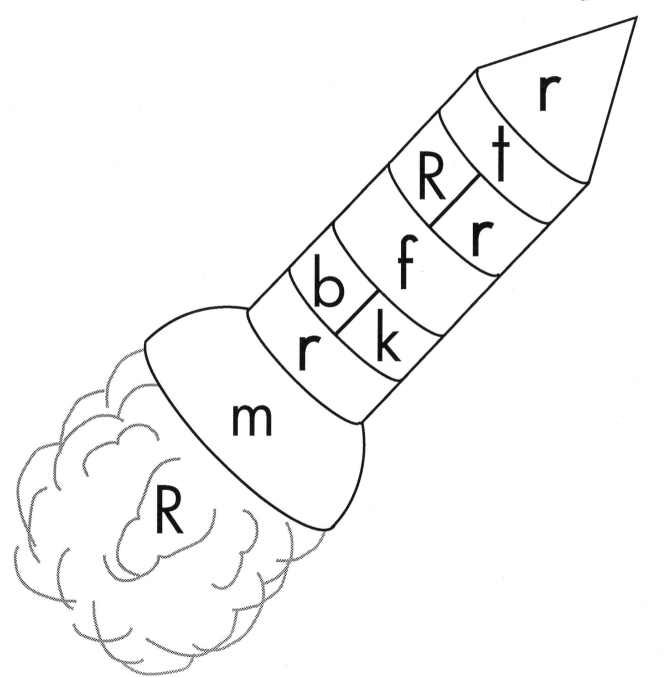

Rr

Teacher: Read the directions aloud while the students listen and work on page 71.

1. I am thinking of something that you can listen to. You may hear music, the news, or a weather report. What am I thinking of? What sound does **radio** begin with? Draw a circle around the **radio**.

2. I am thinking of an animal with long ears and a small, fuzzy tail. This animal hops and its babies are often called bunnies. What is this animal called? What sound do you hear at the beginning of **rabbit**? Draw a carrot in front of the **rabbit**.

3. What would you use to tie up a boat? to swing from a tree? to pull something heavy? I am thinking of a _____. What sound does **rope** begin with? Make the **rope** look like a snake.

4. Sometimes the sun goes behind the clouds and suddenly you feel drops falling. What are these drops? What sound do you hear at the beginning of **rain**? Color the clouds, but not the **rain**.

5. I am thinking of something you can wear on your finger. When it has a diamond or other jewel in it, it sparkles. What is this piece of jewelry called? Say the sound you hear at the beginning of **ring**. Draw a box around the **ring**.

6. You use this to collect leaves into a pile in the fall and to clean out gardens in the spring. What is this tool called? What sound does **rake** begin with? Have you ever used a **rake**? Color its handle.

7. One of the pictures shows something shooting into the air at high speed. Its name begins with /r/. What is it? Say the beginning sound of **rocket** aloud. Then color the **rocket** red, white, and blue.

8. The last picture shows something we don't see very often. Sometimes the sun comes out while it is raining, and a beautiful, colored reflection is seen in the sky. Some people think there is a pot of gold at the end of it. What is this multicolored vision called? What sound does **rainbow** begin with? Color the **rainbow** many beautiful colors.

Listen; then follow the directions.

Color each picture whose name begins with **r** as in .

Follow the arrows to write the letter **r**, which says /**r**/ as in 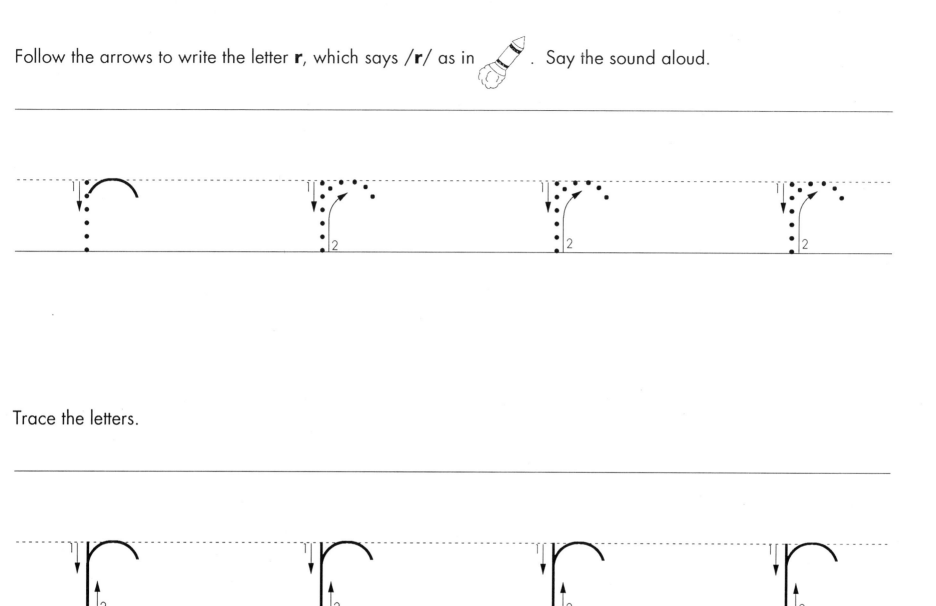 . Say the sound aloud.

Trace the letters.

Which letter does the picture's name begin with? Circle it.

Trace the letters.

Copy the letter.

"X" each picture whose name begins with **r**. Write **r** below those pictures.

Draw a line from each picture to the letter that begins its name.

Say the name of the picture and the sound of its first letter.	Find the letter. Circle it.	Write the letter.
	b r t	
	k b r	
	m r b	
	f m r	
	t r k	

Which sound does the word begin with? Write the letter that stands for the sound.